COUNTRY EXPLORERS

CANADA

Janice Hamilton

Lerner Books • London • New York • Minneapolis

First published in the United Kingdom in 2009 by
Lerner Books,
Dalton House,
60 Windsor Avenue,
London SW19 2RR

Website address: www.lernerbooks.co.uk

This edition was updated and edited for UK publication by Discovery Books Ltd.,
Unit 3, 37 Watling Street, Leintwardine, Shropshire SY7 0LW

Words in **bold** type are explained in the glossary on page 46.

British Library Cataloguing in Publication Data

Hamilton, Janice
Canada. - (Country explorers)
1. Canada - Juvenile literature
i. Title
971'.07

ISBN-13: 978 1 58013 487 3

Printed in Singapore

Table of Contents

Welcome!

Canada is a huge country. It is part of the **continent** of North America. Take a look at the map. Can you name the two things that touch Canada? If you guessed water and the United States, you are right.

The Atlantic Ocean splashes Canada's eastern side. The chilly Arctic Ocean lies to the north. The Pacific Ocean washes against Canada's western shore. The United States of America meets Canada's southern and north-western borders.

Map Whiz Quiz

Trace the outline of the map on pages four and five. In the Atlantic Ocean, put an *E* for 'east'. Write an *S* for 'south' in the USA. The *W* for 'west' goes in the Pacific Ocean. At the squiggly top, put an *N* for 'north' Pick out two colours – one for the USA. Use the other one for all the water around Canada.

ARCTIC
OCEAN

ATLANTIC
OCEAN

PACIFIC
OCEAN

HUDSON
BAY

NEWFOUNDLAND

BAFFIN
ISLAND

NUNAVUT

YUKON

ALBERTA

SASKATCHEWAN

MANITOBA

ONTARIO

QUEBEC

BRITISH
COLUMBIA

Calgary

Vancouver

TRANS CANADA HIGHWAY

LAKE SUPERIOR

DETROIT RIVER

LAKE HURON

Toronto

LAKE MICHIGAN

ST. CLAIR RIVER

LAKE ERIE

LAKE ONTARIO

Montreal

★ Ottawa

PRINCE
EDWARD
ISLAND

NEW
BRUNSWICK

NOVA
SCOTIA

Canada

UNITED STATES

KILOMETRES

0   600

0   500

MILES

N

5

▲ mountains

■ plains

■ lowlands

■ Canadian shield

★ country's capital

• cities

From the East

Fishing villages dot Canada's eastern coast where small numbers of people live.

Peggy's Cove is a fishing village in Nova Scotia. Some people still make a living by catching and selling lobsters there.

More Canadians live in the south-east **lowlands** than anywhere else. Lowland farmers grow fruit and vegetables and raise chickens and cows. Much of Canada's land is on the Canadian Shield. The land is rocky and flat with lots of lakes, streams and swamps. Lots of dinosaur bones have been found there!

Dairy cows graze on a farm in Ontario.

Cascade Mountain towers above the town of Banff in Alberta.

To the West

Moving west from the Canadian Shield, the flat, rocky land gives way to the **Great Plains**. Cows love it here! They have lots of space to roam around and plenty of grass to eat. If you keep going west, the land rises up. You can see the giant peaks of the Western Cordillera. It is a large **mountain range**. Do not go too far west. You will end up in the Pacific Ocean!

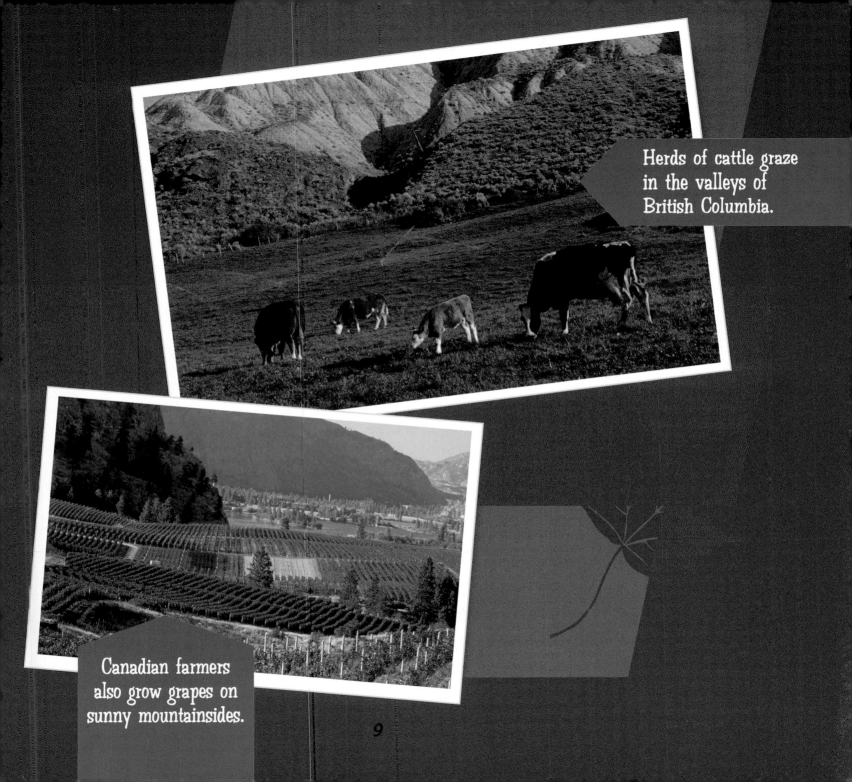

Herds of cattle graze in the valleys of British Columbia.

Canadian farmers also grow grapes on sunny mountainsides.

Lots of Water

If you were to try to count all of the lakes in Canada, it would take a long time. But if you guessed two million, you would be pretty close. Some lakes are very small. Others are the perfect size for fishing and swimming. Five - called the Great Lakes - are so huge you cannot see the other side. See if you can remember their names.

Lots of lakes mean great fishing for everyone!

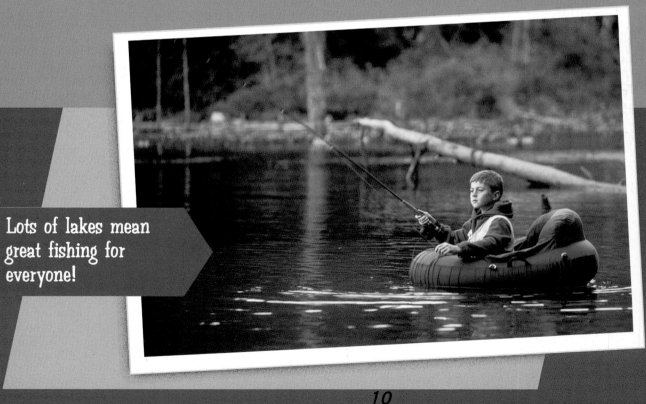

Beautiful ice formations line the shores of Lake Superior in winter.

Deep Water

Lake Superior is the largest freshwater lake in the entire world! It is also the deepest of the Great Lakes. It is so deep that only parts of Lake Superior freeze completely in the winter.

They are Lakes Superior, Huron, Erie, Ontario and Michigan. Canada and the USA share the Great Lakes - except for Lake Michigan. It sits only in the USA.

11

Weather

Brrr! Canadians have to wrap up in winter. Temperatures in many places can dip very low. Winter brings ice and snow. It is a good thing Canadian children like to skate and sledge.

Because Canada is so far north, summers are short. But they are usually warm and sunny. Most summer days are perfect for a walk in the mountains or for fishing and swimming in the lakes.

Slow Movers

In northern Canada, you will see lots of glaciers. Glaciers are huge sheets of ice. They formed because ice and snow piled up for thousands of years. Every time snow does not melt after a storm, more layers of ice build up. The glaciers creep along as they thaw and freeze every season.

The Athabasca Glacier fills this valley.

Visitors to Stay

Explorers from Europe landed long ago on Canada's shores. Soon they were followed by French and British settlers. They came to find good fishing and hunting.

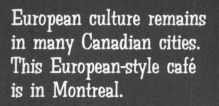

European culture remains in many Canadian cities. This European-style café is in Montreal.

The Gate of Harmonious Interest welcomes visitors to Chinatown in Victoria, British Columbia.

These days, the French and British make up Canada's two biggest **ethnic groups**. Much later, people came from China, Italy, Poland, Jamaica and Vietnam. They made new homes in Canada.

Montreal girls dress up for a South American festival.

First Canadians

Canada's first people did not come by ship. They walked! A strip of land used to stretch from the continent of Asia to North America. Thousands of years ago, people used this strip as a land bridge. They crossed into Canada. They hunted, fished and collected fruits.

An Inuit mother carries her baby in the hood of her warm coat.

In the south, they lived in houses made of tree bark or animal skins. In the north, people built houses of snow, called **igloos**. Canadian Indians and Inuit are the modern day relatives of the earliest Canadians.

This Inuit man is making an igloo by laying blocks of snow in a spiral pattern.

These Canadian Plains Indians appear in traditional dress.

Busy Cities

Ottawa is the capital of Canada. But most Canadians live in one of three big cities - Toronto, Montreal or Vancouver.

Dear Aunt Alice,

Today we skated on the world's longest skating rink. (I only fell a couple of times!) The skating rink is actually the Rideau Canal in Ottawa. A canal is a man-made river. Rideau Canal is eight kilometres long, so we did not skate the whole thing.

They are celebrating Winterlude here. We watched the ice sculpting contest and dogsled races.

See you soon!

Your Fr___
Your T___
Anywh___

Rideau Canal

Toronto is a busy city on the edge of Lake Ontario. Montreal, in the east, was built around a mountain on an island. Vancouver is right next to the Pacific Ocean. People go the seafront to swim or to picnic while watching big ships sail past.

The Toronto skyline lights up at night.

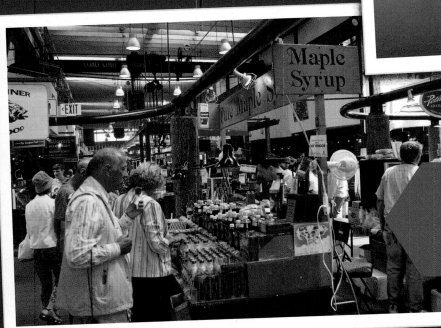

People can buy fresh food and homemade maple syrup at this market in Vancouver.

Two Languages

What's for breakfast? Capitaine Crounche (Captain Crunch)! Cereal boxes in Canada are printed with both French and English words. That is because Canadians speak two **national languages**. Most people in Canada speak English. But people in the **province** of Quebec – as well as in other, smaller communities – speak and write in French. Almost all the children in Quebec go to French *écoles,* or schools.

This bus carries students in Montreal, Quebec. Almost every sign there is written in French.

People from Quebec are Canadians. But many of them would like to have their own country called – what else? – Quebec. Many Québecois (French for 'people from Quebec') are relatives of the first French settlers. Many Canadians from other parts of Canada are relatives of the first British settlers. The Québecois do not want to lose their ties to French culture and language.

This mural is in the old part of the city of Quebec. It shows scenes from the history of the city.

Getting Around

Canadians love to drive. But with all that water in Canada, they sometimes need to take boats. A ferry is a flat boat that carries cars and people across water. Some ferry rides are short, others are six hours long. You'd have time to eat your lunch, read a book and take a nap!

Can't drive across? Cars drive off the deck of a ferry.

From Here to There

One way to travel Canada from coast to coast is by the Trans-Canada Highway. This road is 8,000 kilometres (5,000 miles) long. It goes over and under rivers and lakes. Cars cross bridges and go through tunnels to get across water. Once in a while, travellers get to take a ferry to reach the other side.

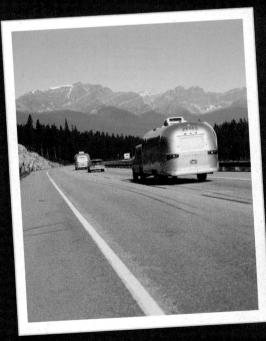

Family Life

Lots of Canadian families live in cities, where space is scarce. But others have homes in the country, where children have plenty of room to play.

Vancouver is a city in British Columbia. This family climbed Cypress Mountain to get a look at the city.

Children play in the remote North-west Territories of Canada.

Family Words

Here are the English and French words for family members.

grandfather grandpapa
grandmother grandmaman
father papa
mother maman
uncle oncle
aunt tante
son fils
daughter fille
brother frère
sister soeur

Two sisters explore a beach near Vancouver.

Fiddleheads are the young, curled-up leaves of the ostrich fern.

What Is Cooking?

Some Canadian food may sound strange. Many Canadians eat the tender shoots of ferns, called fiddleheads. Caribou meat and arctic char (a fish) are some foods on a Canadian menu. Canadian maple syrup shows up on many breakfast tables.

FISH

CARIBOU

Shops sell buffalo and caribou meat as well as beef.

French Toast

Pure maple syrup is best served over a plate of hot French toast. Ask an adult to make you this meal one morning.

What you need:

2 eggs	maple syrup
60 ml milk	butter or margarine
4 slices of bread	

What to do:

Break the eggs into a dish with a wide bottom. Beat the eggs with a fork. Add the milk and beat some more. Melt butter or margarine in a frying pan. Set a slice of bread in the milk mixture, coating both sides. Put soaked bread in pan and cook until it turns golden brown. Turn it over and cook the other side. Repeat with other slices, adding butter or margarine to the pan as needed. Serve with maple syrup. Mmm, mmm, good!

Maple syrup is made from tree sap. Sap is collected in the spring.

School Time

Canadian children start school when they are five years old.
They learn reading, writing, maths, social studies and science.
Some children stay after school for fun activities.

Children on Baffin Island attend this secondary school. Most of the students there are Inuit.

Football is popular with children of all ages. These teams are from Montreal schools.

A student practises at the National Ballet School in Toronto.

Children might try ballet or arts and crafts. Most children go to free state schools. But parents may pay to send their children to private schools. These may offer special programmes. Either way, all children have to do homework.

Sport

She shoots! She scores! Canadians are crazy about hockey. Children play whenever they can. Indoor and outdoor rinks allow children to play in any season. During the winter, Canadians ski and snowboard. Summer means swimming, walking, camping and cycling.

Curling

Curling became an official sport of the Winter Olympics in 1998. The object of curling is to slide a large, round stone across a narrow ice rink. The team that gets the stone closest to a circle at the end of the rink wins. Each player on the four-member team has a different job to help the stone get to the target.

Curlers slide a curling stone across the ice. The stone is a smooth granite rock with a handle attached to it.

Religion

When the French and the British came to Canada, they brought their own customs, languages and religions. Most Canadians are Roman Catholic or Protestant.

Saint Jude's Cathedral in Iqaluit was built to look like an igloo.

32

Those are the main religions of France and Great Britain. But some Canadians belong to other religions too. The number of Muslims and Jews is growing. Canada's Indians and Inuit believe that all people, animals and plants have spirits watching over them.

Holy Blossom Temple is the home of the first Jewish congregation in Ontario.

Holidays

Canadians love holidays. Whoopee! One of the biggest national holidays is Canada Day on 1 July. On that day, Canadians celebrate their country's decision to make one nation out of many provinces.

Different ethnic groups show their patriotism in Canada Day parades. This Chinese dragon is from Victoria.

34

Quebec National Holiday

Canadians living in Quebec celebrate on 24 June. This holiday used to be called Saint Jean Baptiste Day. But in 1977, it officially became the Quebec National Holiday. People proudly wave the blue and white flag of Quebec Province.

On Canada Day and most Canadian holidays, people enjoy picnics, parades and fireworks.

A Québecois cowboy ropes a calf from horseback.

Festivals

Party time! Members of Canada's many ethnic groups celebrate their different cultures during festivals. The French Canadians of Quebec hold the world's only French **rodeo**.

Children march in the Montreal Caribbean Festival Parade.

During Gaelic Mod, Canada's Scottish people play music and have contests. The haunting music of the bagpipes drifts over the crowd. Meanwhile people compete to see who can throw a wooden pole the furthest. Canada's native peoples test their strength and skill during the Northern Games. They compete at drumming, pole twisting and arm wrestling.

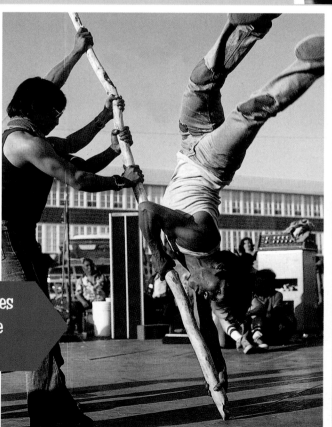

An Inuit man competes in pole twisting in the Northern Games.

Kiawak Ashoona is a famous Inuit artist. He lives in Cape Dorset, a town in Nunavut.

Art

Canada's scenery has moved many artists to draw and paint, but not all art is on a canvas. Many years ago, Canada's Inuit people carved tools and toys out of animal bones and animal horns. You can see some of these artefacts in museums. Modern day Inuit artists carve figures of animals and people out of a soft rock called soapstone.

Totem Poles

Canada's native peoples are famous for their totem poles. They usually carve animal faces – one on top of another – into logs. Each family has its own pole. Native peoples gave meanings to certain animals. That way, people can 'read' another family's pole. What animals would your family's totem pole have?

Story Time

Children laugh out loud when they read Canadian author Robert Munsch's book, *I Have to Go!* It is a funny story about a little boy who remembers to go to the toilet after he puts on his snowsuit.

Another Canadian writer, Paulette Bourgeois, writes tales about Franklin the Turtle. He helps children learn how to share and how to be brave in the dark.

Robert Munsch started telling stories when he worked at a day care centre.

Telling Stories

A great many years ago — before stories were written down — native peoples said the stories out loud to one another. Grandparents told them to their grandchildren. Here is one they may have told while sitting around the fire at night. It is one of the many stories of how the world began.

In the beginning, there were no people. Only one piece of land existed and Sea Lion owned it. The rest of the world was water. Crow stole Sea Lion's baby. Crow would not give the baby back until Sea Lion gave him some sand. Crow sprinkled the sand over the water to create the world. Crow was lonely, though. So he carved Man and Woman from a tree and gave them life.

Sing a Song

Raffi is a popular singer in Canada. He sings songs in French and English. Many Canadians know all the words to 'Big Beautiful Planet' and 'Frére Jacques'.

Canadians like moving to the beat. They dance to country, folk and rock and roll. If their legs get tired, Canadians sit down and listen to the **symphony** or enjoy an **opera**.

Rock musician Alanis Morissette was born in Ottawa.

Row, Row, Row

Have you ever sung songs to make a car journey seem shorter? When the French first came to Canada, they travelled long distances by canoe. To help them keep paddling, they sang song after song – loudly!

These modern people learn about Canada's history by pretending to be French traders and explorers.

THE FLAG OF CANADA

Canada's flag has a red, eleven-pointed maple leaf. It sits on a white background in the centre of the flag. The maple leaf is a national symbol of the country. Vertical, red panels are on either side of the white centre.

FAST FACTS

FULL COUNTRY NAME: Canada

AREA: 9,970,610 square kilometres (3,849,674 square miles9,) or as big as Europe

CAPITAL CITY: Ottawa

OFFICIAL LANGUAGES: English and French

POPULATION: about 32,636,294

SOME MAJOR LANDFORMS:

MOUNTAINS: Canadian Rockies, Coast Mountains and Saint Elias Mountains Canada's highest mountain: Mount Logan.

RIVERS: Churchill, Columbia, Detroit, Fraser, Hayes, Mackenzie, Nelson, Niagara, Saint Clair, Saint Lawrence, Saint Marys, Severn, Thelon, Winisk, Yukon

MAJOR LAND AREAS: the Interior Plateau (an area of plains, river valleys and small mountains), the Arctic Islands (islands in the Arctic Ocean), the Interior Plains, The Canadian Shield (low, rocky hills), the lowlands of Hudson Bay and Saint Lawrence and the Appalachian Region

ANIMALS AND THEIR HABITATS:

FORESTS: bears, deer, elk, mink, moose, mountain lions, rabbits, raccoons, squirrels and wolves

RIVERS: trout, salmon

TUNDRAS: caribou and musk oxen

ARCTIC ISLANDS: arctic foxes and hares, insects, lemmings, polar bears, ptarmigan, seals and walruses

OCEAN: Whales

Glossary

continent: any one of seven large areas of land. The continents are Africa, Antarctica, Asia, Australia, Europe, North America and South America.

ethnic groups: groups of people with many things in common, such as language, religion and customs

igloos: shelters made from blocks of snow

lowlands: flat lands that are lower than the surrounding area

mountain range: a series, or group, of mountains - the parts of the Earth's surface that rise high into the sky

national languages: languages spoken by most people of a country

opera: a play in which the actors sing instead of speak their parts

plains: large areas of flat land

province: a region within a country. A province can make decisions for some types of activities but must follow laws that apply to the whole country.

rodeo: an event that includes contests on horseback. Rodeo events include roping calves and riding bulls.

symphony: a musical piece for large orchestra. Symphony musicians often play stringed instruments (such as violins), wind instruments (such as flutes or clarinets), brass (such as trumpets) and percussion (such as drums).

To Learn More

BOOKS

Blades, Heather. *Canada* (World in Focus) Hodder Wayland, 2006.

Garrington, Sally. *Canada* (Countries of the World) Evans Brothers Ltd., 2005.

Little, Catherine and D'Arcy Little. *The Changing Face of Canada* (Changing Face Of...) Hodder Wayland 2002.

Morris, Neil. *Living in the Arctic* (World Cultures) Raintree, 2007.

WEBSITES

Time for Kids/Go Places: Canada
http://www.timeforkids.com/TFK/teachers/aw/ns/main/0,28132,537729,00.html
Visit Canada's most famous places, travel through Canadian history and even send a postcard to a friend.

Canada for Kids
http://www.pocanticohills.org/canada/canada.htm
Visit the provinces and connect with other sites on this website developed by an elementary school in Sleepy Hollow, New York.

Confederation for Kids
http://www.collectionscanada.ca/confederation/kids/h2-1250-e.html
Learn how Canada became a country, meet famous people in Canadian history, and more.

INDEX

The photographs in this book are used with the permission of: © George Hunter/SuperStock, p 6; © Karl Kummels/SuperStock, pp 7, 23 (left); © Robert Fried Photography/www.robertfriedphotography.com, pp 8, 15 (top); © Chris Cheadle/Alamy, p 9 (top); © T. Vandersar/SuperStock, p 9 (bottom); © britishcolumbiaphotos.com/Alamy, p 10; © Lori Fox Rossi, p 11; © Philip & Karen Smith/SuperStock, p 12; © Dennis Hallinan/Alamy, p 13; © Jon Arnold Images Ltd/Alamy, p 14; © Earl & Nazima Kowall/CORBIS, p 15 (bottom); © SuperStock, Inc./SuperStock, pp 16, 23 (right); © Norman Price/Art Directors, pp 17 (left), 25 (top), 28, 32; © Tim Graham/Alamy, p 17 (right); © Bettmann/CORBIS, p 18; © Toronto Tourism, p 19 (top); © Kari Niemeläinen/Alamy, p 19 (bottom); © age fotostock/SuperStock, pp 20, 21 (right), 25 (bottom); © Richard Cummins/SuperStock, p 21 (left); © Lyn Hancock, pp 22, 26 (right), 37 (bottom); © Reuters/CORBIS, pp 24, 34 (left); © Leroy Simon/Visuals Unlimited, p 26 (left); © Ned Therrien/Visuals Unlimited, p 27; © Megapress/Alamy, p 29 (top); © Paul A. Souders/CORBIS, p 29 (bottom); © AGStockUSA, Inc./Alamy, p 30; © Prisma/SuperStock, p 31; CP/Toronto Star, p 33; © Shaun Cunningham/Alamy, p 34 (right); © Wayne Walton/Lonely Planet Images/Getty Images, p 35 (top); © Rolf Richardson/Alamy, p 35 (bottom); © Tibor Bognar/Art Directors, p 36 (top); © Tibor Bognar/Alamy, p 36 (bottom); © ImageState/Alamy, p 37 (top); © Bryan & Cherry Alexander Photography/Alamy, p 38; © Steve Vidler/SuperStock, p 39; AP Photo, p 40; © Gunter Marx Photography/CORBIS, p 41; © Frank Micelotta/Getty Images, p 42; © Lowell Georgia/CORBIS, p 43. Front cover: © Gunter Marx Photography/CORBIS.
Illustrations by © Bill Hauser/Independent Picture Service

This book was first published in the United States of America in 2008.
Text copyright © 2008 by Lerner Publishing Group, Inc.